FOOTBALL SUPERSTARS

ZLATAN

RULES

SIMON MUGFORD   DAN GREEN

CONTENTS

CHAPTER 1 – **THE MAN ZLATAN**......................................5

CHAPTER 2 – **MALMÖ MEAN STREETS**.........................13

CHAPTER 3 – **KICKS AND TRICKS**................................23

CHAPTER 4 – **ONE OF A KIND!**......................................37

CHAPTER 5 – **BIG TIME**..45

CHAPTER 6 – **IBRA ITALIA**...55

CHAPTER 7 – **SUPER SWEDE**.......................................65

CHAPTER 8 – **BARCA-LOANER**.....................................79

CHAPTER 9 – **PARIS SAINT-ZLATAN**............................87

CHAPTER 10 – **GOING GLOBAL**....................................97

CHAPTER 11 – **PLANET ZLATAN**.................................111

ZLATAN! ZLATAN!

Watch out - it's the football force that is

ZLATAN IBRAHIMOVIĆ!

The incredible **Swedish** superstar striker has played for **EIGHT** of the world's biggest clubs and won more than **30 TROPHIES** in a career that spans over **20 years**.

There is **no-one quite like Zlatan** -

and this book is all about him!

SO, WHAT MAKES **ZLATAN** SUCH A GOOD PLAYER?

Strength
His strong, powerful presence intimidates his opponents.

Height
He towers over the oppositon as the perfect target man.

Acrobatics
Amazing aerial ability, he often scores with a spectacular volley.

Dead–ball king
Excellent at penalties and super-powerful free kicks.

Longevity
23 seasons in top-flight football and still at the top of his game.

ZLATAN IN NUMBERS

A special player like **Zlatan** has some awesome **numbers.**

13 . . . LEAGUE CHAMPIONSHIP wins

17 . . . DOMESTIC CUP wins

504 . . . CLUB GOALS

118 . . . CAPS and

62 GOALS for Sweden

3 . . . SERIE A FOOTBALLER OF THE YEAR awards

1 . . . UEFA EUROPA LEAGUE win

7 . . . CAREER TRANSFERS worth

£150 MILLION

More than

50 MILLION

followers on Instagram!

ZLATAN I.D.

NAME: *Zlatan Ibrahimović*

NICKNAME: *The Lion, Ibra, Ibracadabra*

DATE OF BIRTH: *3 October 1981*

PLACE OF BIRTH: *Malmö, Sweden*

HEIGHT: *1.95 m*

POSITION: *Striker*

CLUBS: *Malmö FF, Ajax, Juventus, Inter Milan, Barcelona, AC Milan (2010-12) Paris Saint-Germain, Manchester United, LA Galaxy, AC Milan (2020-)*

NATIONAL TEAM: *Sweden*

LEFT OR RIGHT-FOOTED: *Both*

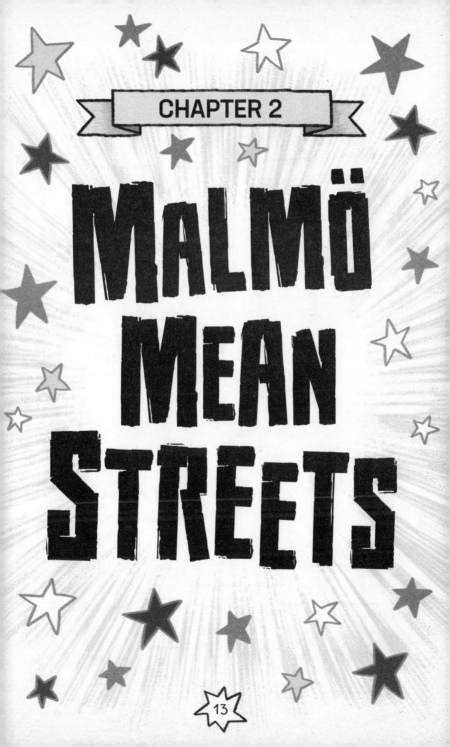

CHAPTER 2

MALMÖ MEAN STREETS

Zlatan Ibrahimović was born in the city of

Malmö, Sweden, in **1981.**

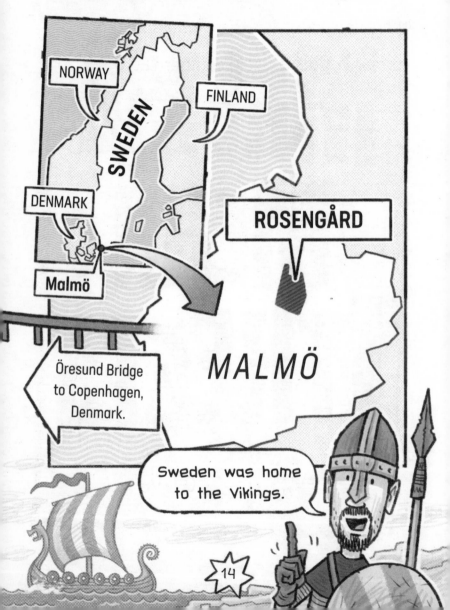

Zlatan lived in an area of the city called **Rosengård.** Lots of the families that lived there, including Zlatan's, came from the former **Yugoslavia** in southern Europe.

Baby Zlatan

1981

Rosengård could be a **tough place** to grow up and it was especially tough for Zlatan.

His parents **divorced** when he was little and at first he lived with his mum and **FIVE** other kids, including his **sister.**

It was **difficult** at home, so Zlatan went to live with his **dad** when he was **nine**.

Zlatan's dad **worked very hard** and there was often more beer than food in the fridge. But he did his best to **look after** Zlatan.

Zlatan would go back to his mum's house for a *good meal!*

Zlatan spent most of his time hanging out with his **mates.** Sometimes that meant **playing football . . .**

Zlatan would often **skip school** and get into all sorts of **trouble.** He and his friends would do really stupid stuff like **steal bikes** and **throw fireworks**.

The tough neighbourhood was making him a **tough kid.** Zlatan would get **angry** and get into **fights.**

"YOU CAN TAKE THE GUY FROM ROSENGÅRD BUT YOU CAN'T TAKE ROSENGÅRD FROM THE GUY."

Zlatan Ibrahimović

22

In the estates in Rosengård, Zlatan and his mates played football on small, **rough pitches.**

He learned to be **fast, quick** and **tough.**

It was good to win, but for Zlatan, it was even better to do it with some **fancy tricks**.

Zlatan practised as many **football skills** and **tricks** as he could.

He loved to **dribble** . . .

He tried out **feints** and **stepovers** . . .

STEP!

Cheeky **backheels** . . .

DUMF!

And spectacular **bicycle kicks** . . .

POW!

27

Zlatan's football **heroes** were strikers who played with **flair** and had **slick tricks**.

The Brazilian stars **Romario . . .**

Scored more than 1000 goals, starred at PSV Eindhoven and Barcelona

When he was **six,** Zlatan started playing for a local club called **MBI.** He worked hard to show off his skills but his bad temper often got him into **trouble.**

Zlatan decided that MBI was full of **'snobby Swedes'** so he moved to **FBK Balkan,** a side founded by the Yugoslav immigrants in Rosengård.

But he fell out with **FBK** as well!

In the end, he switched between both clubs, riding a (usually stolen) bike to training.

OI, THAT'S MY BIKE!

Zlatan loved watching Kung Fu films with his dad. **Bruce Lee** and **Jackie Chan** were his heroes.

They watched old boxing matches together, too. Zlatan's idol was **Muhammad Ali.**

Zlatan started practising the martial art **Taekwondo** as a teenager, later becoming a **black belt.**

KA-BLAM!

Perhaps all those *flying kicks* shaped his playing style on the pitch?

35

"THE ONLY THING HE WANTED WAS TO SCORE GOALS, SO SOMETIMES HE LISTENED TO THE COACHES BUT SOMETIMES HE JUST DID WHAT HE WANTED."

Ivan Milosević, who played with Zlatan at FBK Balkan

CHAPTER 4

ONE OF A KIND!

Zlatan is a **unique** character in football - a little bit crazy, wild and **LOVES** talking about himself.

"I CAN'T HELP BUT LAUGH AT HOW PERFECT I AM."

BUT HE'S NOT ENTIRELY ALONE. WHO ARE FOOTBALL'S OTHER FAMOUS **BAD BOYS?**

MARIO BALOTELLI

2005-PRESENT

NATIONAL TEAM: **ITALY**

POSITION: **STRIKER**

'Super Mario' played alongside Zlatan at Inter Milan, where **José Mourinho** described him as **unmanageable.**

Balotelli once set off **fireworks** in his own house and, according to legend, gave money to strangers in **Manchester** while a City player.

WHY ALWAYS ME?

LUIS SUÁREZ

2005-PRESENT

NATIONAL TEAM: **URUGUAY**

POSITION: **STRIKER**

Suárez was a sensation alongside Messi and Neymar at Barcelona. But he's also an ace at **diving** for penalties and most bizarrely - **BITING** his opponents.

WHAT I CAN SAY? I GET HUNGRY DURING A MATCH!

40

ROY KEANE

1989-2006

NATIONAL TEAM: **IRELAND**

POSITION: **MIDFIELDER**

Now he's a dog-loving TV pundit, but the Manchester United legend was a midfield maniac who was infamously sent home from the 2002 World Cup after a **big bust-up** with his Ireland boss Mick McCarthy.

VINNIE JONES

1984-1999

NATIONAL TEAM: **WALES**

POSITION: **MIDFIELDER**

Vinnie was the self-styled **'hard man'** and the leader of the **'Crazy Gang'** at Wimbledon, whose rough, aggressive style beat Liverpool in the 1988 FA Cup.

He went on to play tough guys as a *Hollywood actor!*

Just a little more make-up Mr Jones.

GRR!

VINNIE

ERIC CANTONA

1983-1997

NATIONAL TEAM: **FRANCE**

POSITION: **FORWARD**

'King Eric' is a Manchester United and Premier League legend but infamous for the Zlatan-style **flying kick** he launched against a Crystal Palace fan in 1995 that led to a **lengthy ban.** Cantona also became an **actor!**

"I AM NOT A MAN, I AM **CANTONA!**"

43

DIEGO MARADONA

1976-1997

NATIONAL TEAM: **ARGENTINA**

POSITION:
MIDFIELDER / STRIKER

The Argentine legend famously scored with his **hand** against England in the 1986 World Cup. He was banned for **fighting** and many other reasons but is arguably the **greatest player** of all time.

He famously called his handball goal *The Hand of God*

44

Zlatan was 13 when he joined the youth team at **Malmö FF.** It was a proper, professional club that played in the **Allsvenskan** - the top Swedish league.

But Zlatan didn't care about that. He carried on with his **tricks** and **hated training.**

The parents of the other boys wanted Zlatan **out of the club**.

He nearly quit himself.

But the coaches knew he was **special** and got him to **stay.**

Zlatan made his **debut** for the first team in **September 1999** and scored his first goal on the last day of the season.

But then **Malmö** were **relegated** for the first time in their history!

The following season, Zlatan scored **12 GOALS** to help Malmö get promoted.

His attitude and style was getting him **noticed.**

Back in the Allsvenskan, **19-year-old** Zlatan was Sweden's hottest young player.

Arsenal offered him a trial.

IBRA DOESN'T DO TRIALS.

In **July 2001**, Zlatan signed for the top Dutch side **Ajax** for **£7 million.** He celebrated by buying a Mercedes.

ZOOM!!

But Zlatan spent a lot of his first season at Ajax on the bench.

Then in **2002–03,** Zlatan scored **21 goals,** including **FIVE** in the **Champions League.**

GREATEST GOAL #1

22 AUGUST 2004

EREDIVISIE

AJAX 6-2 NAC BREDA

Zlatan cancelled out Breda's early goal but his second was **truly special.**

An awesome **SOLO RUN** where he beat five players and slotted home -

He was compared to **Maradona** and **Zinedine Zidane**!

Zlatan won the Eredivisie **TWICE** at Ajax.

ZLATAN AT MALMÖ

SEASON	GAMES	GOALS	ASSISTS
1999	6	1	-
2000	29	14	-
2001	12	3	-
TOTAL	47	18	-

ZLATAN AT AJAX

SEASON	GAMES	GOALS	ASSISTS
2001-02	33	9	5
2002-03	42	21	3
2003-04	31	15	8
2004-05	4	3	1
TOTAL	110	48	17

Zlatan signed for Serie A giants **Juventus** in 2004 for **£14.5 MILLION.** He joined a team of superstars including:

French super striker
David Trezeguet . . .

Czech midfield master
Pavel Nedvěd . . .

Legendary Italian forward
Alessandro Del Piero . . .

Italy's star goalkeeper
Gianluigi Buffon . . .

and **Fabio Capello** was
the tough-guy manager.

57

Zlatan scored **16 GOALS** in his first season at Juve and won the **Serie A Foreign Footballer of the Year** award.

Zlatan won **Serie A** twice, but Juventus was later found to be cheating. The title wins were removed and the club was relegated.

So Zlatan moved on!

Mino Raiola, Zlatan's agent

WE'RE OFF!

ZLATAN AT JUVENTUS

SEASON	GAMES	GOALS	ASSISTS
2004-05	45	16	10
2005-06	47	10	9
TOTAL	92	26	19

In **2006** Zlatan moved to **Inter Milan** - where his hero Ronaldo had played - for

£22.5 MILLION.

He scored and assisted on his debut and ended the season as **Inter's top scorer** in Serie A, with **15 goals.**

Zlatan won Serie A **three times in a row** with Inter and was named both Serie A Foreign Footballer of the Year AND Serie A Footballer of the Year in **2007–08** and **2008–09**.

GREATEST GOAL #2

4 OCTOBER 2008

SERIE A

INTER MILAN 2-1 BOLOGNA

Zlatan produced the first example of one of his **trademark goals** - an incredible **backheel volley** that left the fans stunned!

This was the Serie A Goal of the Year!

ZLATAN AT INTER MILAN

SEASON	GAMES	GOALS	ASSISTS
2006-07	36	15	9
2007-08	34	22	12
2008-09	47	29	11
TOTAL	117	66	32

"(CRISTIANO) RONALDO IS A GOOD PLAYER BUT HE IS CERTAINLY NOT THE BEST . . . FOR ME, IBRAHIMOVIĆ IS THE BEST."

José Mourinho, Zlatan's manager at Inter and Manchester United.

CHAPTER 7

SUPER SWEDE

Zlatan broke into the Swedish national side while he was still at Malmö. He played for the **under-18s** and **under-21s** before making his senior debut in January 2001 against the **Faroe Islands.**

BAA!

The *Faroe Islands* have more *sheep* than *people!*

BAA!

BAA!

Shortly after signing for Ajax, Zlatan scored his **first goal** for Sweden, against **Azerbaijan** in a 2002 World Cup qualifier.

KRACK!

Zlatan could have played for **Bosnia and Herzegovina** or **Croatia**.

67

ZLATAN is a **LEGEND** in **Swedish** football.

ALL-TIME TOP SCORER
62 GOALS

EUROPEAN CHAMPIONSHIP
TOP SCORER **6 GOALS**

LONGEST NATIONAL CAREER
MORE THAN **20 YEARS!**

CAPTAIN FOR **58 GAMES**

12 SWEDISH FOOTBALLER OF THE YEAR **AWARDS**

More than any other player

15 SWEDISH FORWARD OF THE YEAR **AWARDS**

EURO HIGHLIGHTS

ZLATAN'S BEST MOMENTS AT THE EUROPEAN CHAMPIONSHIPS

18 JUNE 2004

EURO 2004 GROUP STAGE

ITALY 1-1 SWEDEN

His late equaliser was **classic Zlatan** – an awesome back-heel lob that was the **Goal of the Tournament.**

19 JUNE 2012

EURO 2012 GROUP STAGE

SWEDEN 2-0 FRANCE

Zlatan scored with a **SUPERB VOLLEY** *and was named* **Man of the Match.**

BOOM!

17 NOVEMBER 2015

EURO 2016 QUALIFYING PLAY-OFF 2ND LEG

DENMARK 2-2 SWEDEN (2-3 ON AGG)

Zlatan scored both goals to help Sweden qualify for **EURO 2016** *at the expense of Scandinavian rivals Denmark.*

Zlatan retired from international football after **EURO 2016.**

WORLD CUP HIGHLIGHTS

WHOMP!

16 OCTOBER 2012

WORLD CUP 2014 QUALIFIER

GERMANY 4-4 SWEDEN

*Playing away in Berlin, Sweden went 4-0 down, before **Captain Zlatan** inspired a second-half comeback, scoring the first of **FOUR goals**.*

19 NOVEMBER 2013

WORLD CUP 2014
QUALIFYING PLAY-OFF 2ND LEG

SWEDEN 2-3 PORTUGAL (2-4 ON AGG)

*Zlatan vs Ronaldo. Unfortunately Cristiano scored three goals to Zlatan's **TWO** and Sweden did not reach the finals in Brazil.*

In **March 2021** Zlatan announced his return to international football.

ZLATAN TWEET

'The return of the god'

TWEET!

He played a **World Cup 2022** qualifier against Kosovo aged 39 years, 5 months and 25 days – the oldest Swedish player ever!

73

GREATEST GOAL #3

14 NOVEMBER 2012

INTERNATIONAL FRIENDLY

SWEDEN 4-2 ENGLAND

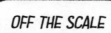
OFF THE SCALE
GENIUS!

KA-POW!

Zlatan was already on a **hat-trick** when, from 30 yards out and with his back to the goal, his acrobatic **bicycle kick** sent the ball into the net. **INCREDIBLE!**

IT'S A WORK OF ART

This goal won the **2013 Puskas Award** for **Goal of the Year.**

75

SWEDISH STARS

Zlatan is Sweden's **greatest** ever player.

Who else is up there with the best?

HENRIK LARSSON

A legend at Celtic, Larsson also played for Barcelona and Man Utd (like Zlatan) and scored 37 goals for Sweden.

GUNNAR GREN

Gren was awesome for AC Milan in the 1950s and a key player for Sweden when they came second at the 1958 World Cup.

GUNNAR NORDAHL

Nordahl played alongside Gren at Milan and is the club's all-time top goalscorer. He scored 43 goals for his country.

FREDDIE LJUNGBERG

Winner of multiple trophies at Arsenal, the wonder winger was also famous for modelling underpants!

Like this?

77

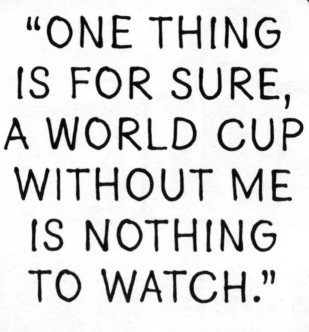

CHAPTER 8

BARCA-LOANER

In the summer of 2009 Zlatan was on the move again, to join the superstars of **BARCELONA . . .**

FEE: £62 MILLION!

The starry squad included . . .

Thierry Henry
(French legend)

Xavi
(master playmaker)

Andrés Iniesta
(midfield wizard)

Gerard Piqué
(defensive rock)

Lionel Messi
(yes, him)

"I WAS PROBABLY WITH THE BEST TEAM IN HISTORY."

ZLATAN'S RECORD AT *BARCELONA*

(ONE SEASON)

- [x] LA LIGA WINNER
- [x] FIFA CLUB WORLD CUP WINNER
- [x] UEFA SUPER CUP WINNER
- [x] SUPERCOPA DE ESPAÑA WINNER X 2
- [x] CHAMPIONS LEAGUE SEMI-FINALIST
- [x] 46 APPEARANCES
- [x] 22 GOALS
- [x] 13 ASSISTS

But then, Zlatan had a **BIG bust-up** with manager **Pep Guardiola.** So he was sent out on loan.

Zlatan was back in Italy. This time with **AC Milan,** the **BIG** rivals of his old club, **Inter.**

ZLATAN'S 2010-11 SEASON AT AC MILAN

Milan's top scorer *(21 goals)*

Scored in the **Milan derby**

Serie A **Footballer of the Year**

Won **Serie A**

This was Zlatan's **FIFTH** Serie A win!

Milan signed him for **£21 MILLION** at the end of the season.

He followed that with **35 goals** and **12 assists** in **2011–12**.

BOOM!

SERIE A TOP SCORER (28 GOALS)

Zlatan's two seasons at Milan saw plenty of **goals, trophies** and **awards . . .**

But there were also **RED CARDS** for fighting and swearing at a referee.

He was suspended for *EIGHT* games in total.

July 2012: another summer transfer window and Zlatan was on the move ... **AGAIN!**

His **£18 MILLION** transfer to **Paris Saint-Germain** was **A VERY BIG DEAL!**

*HELLO, ZLATAN IS HERE

PSG had recently been taken over by new owners who were spending **BIG money** on **superstar players.**

Zlatan was one of the first.

PSG HiGHLiGHTS

ZLATAN'S BIGGEST GAMES IN A PSG SHIRT.

23 OCTOBER 2013

CHAMPIONS LEAGUE GROUP STAGE

ANDERLECHT 0-5 PSG

Wearing the captain's armband, Zlatan scored **FOUR** goals, including a long-range screamer against the Belgian side.

4 OCTOBER 2015

LIGUE 1

PSG 2-1 MARSEILLE

*The PSG-Marseille derby, **Le Classique,** is the biggest fixture in Ligue 1. Zlatan scored **TWO** penalties in **FOUR** minutes to become PSG's all-time top scorer at the time.*

13 MARCH 2016

LIGUE 1

TROYES 0-9 PSG

*Zlatan scored **FOUR** goals. The third was his **100th Ligue 1 goal** and the result won the league for PSG. What a game!*

His first three goals, after **46, 53** and **56 minutes,** is the **fastest hat-trick** in **Ligue 1.**

GREATEST GOAL #4

19 OCTOBER 2013
LIGUE 1
PSG 4-0 BASTIA

Zlatan scored **TWICE** in the opening

15 minutes. The first goal was pure Zlatan

magic – an awesome back-heel volley that

swerved around the **back** of the defender.

C'est fantastique!

SLAP!

Magnifique!

ZLATAN'S PSG AWESOMENESS!

LIGUE 1 TOP SCORER
2012-13
2013-14
2015-16

RECORD LIGUE 1 GOALS IN A SEASON
38 (2015-16)

MOST GOALS BY A PSG PLAYER IN ONE SEASON
(ALL COMPETITIONS)
50 (2015-16)

ALL-TIME TOP SCORER IN LE CLASSIQUE
11 GOALS

PSG'S SECOND-HIGHEST ALL-TIME SCORER
156 GOALS

Edinson Cavani holds the record now.

ZLATAN'S PSG RECORD

SEASON	GAMES	GOALS	ASSISTS
2012-13	46	35	17
2013-14	46	41	17
2014-15	37	30	8
2015-16	51	50	19
TOTAL	180	156	61

"I CAME LIKE A KING, LEFT LIKE A LEGEND"

Zlatan, announcing that he was leaving PSG in 2016.

CHAPTER 10

GOING GLOBAL

Zlatan packed his bags again in **July 2016** and joined **MANCHESTER UNITED** - the **EIGHTH** different club of his career.

FREE TRANSFER

He was joining up with his manager from **Inter Milan, José Mourinho,** who was now the United boss.

In true Zlatan-style, he had an instant impact, scoring the winner in the **Community Shield** as **Leicester City** were beaten **2–1.**

HE WENT ON TO:

score on his **Premier League** debut

score the winner in the **League Cup Final**

become United's **top goalscorer** in 2016-17 (28 goals)

win the **Europa League**

and get a **three-match ban** for violent conduct!

SAME OLD ZLATAN.

ZLATAN'S UNITED RECORD

SEASON	GAMES	GOALS	ASSISTS
2016-17	46	28	10
2017-18	7	1	-
TOTAL	53	29	10

He was injured for most of this season.

WHERE WOULD HE GO NEXT?

In 2018, in true superstar-style, Zlatan moved to **LOS ANGELES**, to play for **LA Galaxy.**

Dear Los Angeles,
you're welcome.

Zlatan Ibrahimović!

He paid for this
advert himself.

Zlatan was following in the footsteps of top European players such as:

Steven Gerrard

Ashley Cole

Robbie Keane

And most famously of all . . .

David Beckham

HOLLYWOOD HIGHLIGHTS

ZLATAN'S BIG GALAXY MOMENTS

31 MARCH 2018

LA GALAXY DEBUT

MAJOR LEAGUE SOCCER

LA GALAXY 4-3 LOS ANGELES FC

*The Galaxy were behind when Zlatan came on as a sub, scored with a long-range **SCREAMER** and won the game with an injury-time winner.*

BAM!

CRAZY!

This was the MLS *Goal of the Season.*

15 SEPTEMBER 2018

MAJOR LEAGUE SOCCER

TORONTO FC 5-3 LA GALAXY

*Zlatan scored the **500th goal** of his career with a perfect back-heel volley.*

16 SEPTEMBER 2019

MAJOR LEAGUE SOCCER

LA GALAXY 7-2 SPORTING KANSAS CITY

*Zlatan scored his third – and final – **hat-trick** for LA Galaxy.*

Zlatan soon hit the **Hollywood big time.**

Everyone loved Zlatan - and he loved appearing

on talk shows - talking about himself!

ZLATAN'S LA GALAXY RECORD

SEASON	GAMES	GOALS	ASSISTS
2018	27	22	7
2019	31	31	8
TOTAL	58	53	15

Zlatan said goodbye to LA in his own unique way:

"THE STORY CONTINUES . . . NOW GO BACK TO WATCH BASEBALL."

At the age of **38,** most footballers have retired. But not Zlatan! In **2019** he was back at **AC Milan** playing at the very highest level.

WHAM!

There were goals . . .

28 in two seasons.

Records . . .

Oldest goalscorer in the Milan Derby.

First player to score **50** Serie A goals for AC Milan AND Inter Milan.

Oldest player to score **10** or more Serie A goals in a season.

And of course, trouble!

ZLATAN AT MILAN

SEASON	GAMES	GOALS	ASSISTS
2010-11	41	21	12
2011-12	44	35	12
2019-20	20	11	5
2020-21	27	17	3
2021-22	8	3	2
TOTAL	140	87	34

"I'M OLD. THAT'S NO SECRET! AGE IS JUST A NUMBER."

110

CHAPTER 11

PLANET ZLATAN

MONEY MONEY MONEY

Big contracts at some of the world's
biggest football clubs have made Zlatan
very wealthy.

He is worth around

£140 MILLION.

Zlatan has sponsorship deals with top **sportswear brands.**

And has advertised everything from **cars** to **deodorant!**

He's helped charities like the **United Nations World Food Programme.**

He also started a **fundraiser** in Italy during the **coronavirus pandemic.**

"IF THE VIRUS DON'T GO TO ZLATAN, ZLATAN GOES TO THE VIRUS."

HUH?

As a kid, Zlatan loved his (and other people's) bikes, but you won't see him riding one today. He has an **awesome** garage of **cars** including . . .

. . . a super-rare *FERRARI MONZA SP2*

A 38th birthday present to *himself!*

HAPPY BIRTHDAY TO ZLATAN, HAPPY BIRTHDAY TO ZLATAN!

VAROOM! VAROOM!

... a **LAMBORGHINI GALLARDO**

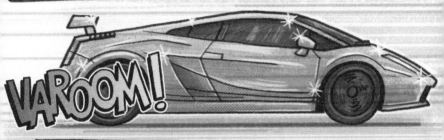

... a **PORSCHE 918 SPYDER**

... and a (sensible, Swedish) **VOLVO XC90!**

MADE IN SWEDEN

Is Zlatan the most **famous person** from **Sweden?** Maybe. He's definitely different than some of the others . . .

Environmental activist, **Greta Thunberg**

SKOLSTREJK
FÖR
KLIMATET

Pop legends, **ABBA**

ZLATAN SAYS . . .

Zlatan **ALWAYS** has something to say. And it's usually outrageous, hilarious or both.

"FIRST I WENT LEFT; HE DID TOO. THEN I WENT RIGHT AND HE DID TOO. THEN I WENT LEFT AGAIN AND HE WENT TO BUY A HOT DOG."

- talking about Liverpool defender Stephane Henchoz

"YOU BOUGHT A **FERRARI,** BUT YOU DRIVE IT LIKE A **FIAT.**"

- on how Pep Guardiola used him at Barcelona

"I DON'T THINK THAT YOU CAN SCORE AS SPECTACULAR A GOAL AS THOSE OF ZLATAN IN A VIDEO GAME."

"ONLY GOD KNOWS . . . YOU'RE TALKING TO HIM NOW."

Zlatan is an **ABSOLUTE LEGEND** in the world of football. Wherever Zlatan goes, there is going to be **excitement, controversy** and . . . **spectacular goals!**

This unique footballer is . . .

. . . the only player to score in the Champions League with **SIX** different teams

. . . the only player to **score on his debut** in the Premier League, La Liga, Serie A, Ligue 1 and the Champions League

. . . the only player to play in the Champions League with **SEVEN** different teams.

ZLAT'S STATS

THERE ISN'T SPACE FOR ALL OF ZLATAN'S HONOURS AND AWARDS, BUT THESE ARE SOME **HIGHLIGHTS!**

EREDIVISIE
2001-02
2003-04

SERIE A
2006-07
2007-08
2008-09
2010-11

LA LIGA
2009-10

LIGUE 1
2012-13
2013-14
2014-15
2015-16

SUPERCOPPA ITALIA
2006
2008
2011

FIFA WORLD CLUB CUP
2009

EUROPA LEAGUE
2016-17

PUSKÁS AWARD
2013

SERIE A FOOTBALLER OF THE YEAR
2007-08
2008-09
2010-11

CAPOCANNONIERE
2008-09
2011-12

LIGUE 1 TOP SCORER
2012-13
2013-14
2015-16

123

QUIZ TIME!

How much do you know about **ZLATAN IBRAHIMOVIĆ?** Try this quiz to find out, then test your friends!

1. At which club did Zlatan begin his career?

---

2. Which Brazilian striker was Zlatan's hero as a kid?

---

3. Zlatan has a black belt in which martial art?

---

4. Which was the first Italian club Zlatan played for?

---

5. How much did Inter Milan pay for Zlatan in 2006?

---

6. How many goals has Zlatan scored for Sweden?

----

7. Zlatan won the Puskás Award in 2013 for an awesome goal against which country?

----

8. Which manager at Barcelona did Zlatan fall out with?

----

9. How many goals did Zlatan score against Anderlecht in the Champions League in 2013?

----

10. When Zlatan said, "The story continues . . . Now go back to watch baseball," which club was he talking about?

The answers are on the next page *but no peeking!*

ANSWERS

1. Malmö FF
2. Ronaldo
3. Taekwondo
4. Juventus
5. £22.5 million

6. 62
7. England
8. Pep Guardiola
9. Four
10. LA Galaxy

ZLATAN IBRAHIMOVIĆ:
WORDS YOU NEED TO KNOW

Eredivisie
The top football league in the Netherlands.

Serie A
The top football league in Italy.

La Liga
The top football league in Spain.

Capocannoniere
Award for the top scorer in a Serie A season

Champions League
European club competition held every year. The winner is the best team in Europe.

Europa League
The second-tier European club competition

Ligue 1
The top football league in France.

Major League Soccer (MLS)
The top football league in the USA.

ABOUT THE AUTHORS

Simon's first job was at the Science Museum, making paper aeroplanes and blowing bubbles big enough for your dad to stand in. Since then he's written all sorts of books about the stuff he likes, from dinosaurs and rockets, to llamas, loud music and of course, football. Simon has supported Ipswich Town since they won the FA Cup in 1978 (it's true - look it up) and once sat next to Rio Ferdinand on a train. He lives in Kent with his wife and daughter, a dog, cat and two tortoises.

Dan has drawn silly pictures since he could hold a crayon. Then he grew up and started making books about stuff like trucks, space, people's jobs, *Doctor Who* and *Star Wars*. Dan remembers Ipswich Town winning the FA Cup but he didn't watch it because he was too busy making a Viking ship out of brown paper. As a result, he knows more about Vikings than football. Dan lives in Suffolk with his wife, son, daughter and a dog that takes him for very long walks.